Makers Ware

Ceramic, Wood and Glass
for the Tabletop

GINGKO PRESS

Makers Ware

Ceramic, Wood and Glass
for the Tabletop

ISBN 978-1-58423-667-2

First Published in 2017 in the USA by
Gingko Press by arrangement with
Sandu Publishing Co., Ltd.

Gingko Press, Inc.
1321 Fifth Street
Berkeley, CA 94710 USA
Tel: (510) 898 1195
Fax: (510) 898 1196
Email: books@gingkopress.com
www.gingkopress.com

Sponsored by Design 360°
– Concept and Design Magazine

Edited and produced by
Sandu Publishing Co., Ltd.

Book design, concepts & art direction by
Sandu Publishing Co., Ltd.
Chief Editor: Wang Shaoqiang
Design Director: Niu Huizhen

info@sandupublishing.com
www.sandupublishing.com

Printed and bound in China

Contents

Foreword
— The First Bowl ? —

I've always held a bowl in my heart, in addition to a precious bowl kept in my house – it represents a personal history of discovering and falling in love. When I was in middle school I used to go to a traditional folk art boutique called "High Mountain Folk Art" every now and then. Miraculously, the boutique is still standing in a narrow lane in Central Hong Kong. I still remember every time I walked by the shop window and saw the stacks of big earthenware bowls with blue flowers, which I couldn't afford. They reminded me of one of Zhang Yimou's movies which begins with a scene of people eating noodles from bowls like those which traditionally could be found in every family in the countryside of Shaanxi Province. Later when I was visiting an art master in Beijing I saw a series of rare earthenware bowls with different patterns in his living room, which made me feel incredibly jealous. Finally and unexpectedly, I bought a bowl at the "high price" of 16 pounds from the Houseware Department of Liberty in London. The Lamian-noodle sized bowl, with its traditional simple shape, gentle color and vivacious pattern is the perfect bowl for me. It was as if I'd discovered a "national treasure"

abroad and returned it to Hong Kong in the mid-1990s.

Four years ago when I was on a road trip from Xi'an to Taiyuan, Shanxi, I was planning to visit Chenlu, an ancient town in Tongchuan City – the production place of this earthenware bowl with blue flowers. But the trip was eventually cancelled for two reasons: one, the town was out of our way, and two, my friend said I would be disappointed if I went because the place was nothing like it used to be. But ever since then I couldn't forget the thought of visiting. Finally, I had the chance to give a lecture in Xi'an and I decided to visit Tongchuan several days before my lecture, even if the trip would ruin my dream.

The two-hour road trip to Chenlu located in the piedmont region was a little bit depressing because of the endless rain. My friend who went with me knew a local old master, thus we went straight to the only workshop in town which was still producing this kind of earthenware bowl with blue flowers. Most of the workshops and factories stopped producing this kind of earthenware bowl because of the small profit. In fact, the workshop we visited was still using the same raw material, the same glazing techniques and the same bowl modeling from long ago. However, the paint quality was no longer as vivid as it used to be, even though it was named the "Best Bowl in the World" by government officials. In the end, I reluctantly bought two of the actually lackluster bowls as a memento.

Holding up this big bowl to represent completeness had finally become too heavy of a burden. The inheritance and renaissance of "folk art" is never an easy thing.

We talk about utensils and food, seeking their relationship to history and putting them into the stories and context of today, provoking emotions deep in our heart. What we call design, lifestyle and attitude, are definitely not the unreal fancy of some designers or creators. These concepts have to be considered against the background of society, politics and economy. That's how a utensil becomes burdened with its unique context, and only then does the food it holds become connected to the actual world. Everyday life and small

happinesses might not become independent concepts over time – maybe I should learn to accept the "evolution" of the earthenware bowl with blue flowers. The worst situation can give rise to an optimistic future.

For this reason I feel grateful to read this survey of utensil and tableware creators from different cultural backgrounds, sharing their profound experience and professional knowledge. It's inspiring to read such a book during the long journey of the folk art renaissance.

— Craig Au Yeung Ying Chai

Artists of the Craft

Knives, forks, spoons, chopsticks, cups,
bowls, saucers; no matter what type of tableware,
are the ideal partner for food.
Our designers have been determinedly exploring
and trying to create tableware that pairs perfectly
with food. Some of them are
focused on special material; others are dedicated
to expressing the best representations
of designs envisioned in their minds.
Nevertheless, all of them are in love with life,
food, and design.
They follow their hearts to create their ware,
which makes it unnecessary
to judge their works.

Artist

Loving
Imperfection

Oji Masanori

With an aim to design for life, he fully immerses himself into design, and discovers the details that offers people warmth, and comfort in everyday life.

Oji Masanori

Japan

Oji Masanori was born in Hiroshima, Japan in 1974. He graduated from Architecture at the Hiroshima Institute of Technology in 1997 and established Oji&Design in 2004. His works have been recognized with the JIDA Dyson Design Award and the 2003 Kokuyo Design Award, to name just a few. www.o-ji.jp

Although the act of eating doesn't fully occupy our lives, it's a very important aspect of them. Oji Masanori says he doesn't have any special eating habits, but eating together with family or friends is his favorite thing in daily life. For his own work, Oji chooses a certain style over material. He likes tableware without strong characteristics, but he intentionally picks pieces for meals that match each other, as well as the food they would be interacting with. Only when the instruments match their food, keeping their own characteristics without stealing the show, can they be called "good utensils," because only then can people feel the soul of the tool while eating the food they're working with. Everything about a utensil, even its texture, has the potential to affect the mood of the person using it. For example, people can feel the warmth of wood through using or even just touching it. Wood has an amiable feeling that eases people's mood, which is a different feeling from ceramic ware. Oji works hard to manage his studio, and his work has already unintentionally become inextricably linked with his life. Though it's hard to separate private time from his work because he often forgets about the time when he's absorbed in creation, Oji tries to spend some quality time resting occasionally. He believes wooden utensils can always pacify taut nerves in his busy work.

Choosing the perfect piece for each dish is one of the most important tasks for every chef, because suitable utensils complete and beautify the dining scene. It is not a surprise that many exquisite and abundant Japanese dishes are presented with basic and simple tableware. But as evidenced by Oji Masanori's design, the natural texture of the material, the details in simple lines, and the delicate crafting technique always bring a pleasant change of atmosphere.

Oji majored in Architecture in college. After graduating and working as an architect, he found that instead of buildings, spaces, and graphic design, he was more interested in and better at creating quality objects. He knows that everyone has his or her own forte, thus he decided to change his career path to specialize in product design and established his own studio. Now he often cooperates with small handicraft product manufacturers for the production of his work, and he handles the entire design process, from product to branding design. The small scale traditional

IHADA brass series, FUTAGAMI

Production process of FUTAGAMI's brass utensils

handicraft industry in Japan is famous around the world for its exquisite craftsmanship and high quality. In Oji's opinion, traditional designs and new designs are closely connected; no one is better than the other. It's only a matter of whether the item is suitable. Whether the work is traditional or new, overproduction can destroy the original beauty of the pieces. The ecosystem created by the designers, manufacturers, retailers, and consumers must develop on the principle of not destroying the overall balance. Thus Oji wants his designs to be produced following a certain rate of progress and in limited quantities with special characteristics and a handcrafted appeal that people can still use in everyday life.

The solutions to certain questions often come with more and more new questions. Oji believes the key to answering these questions in design is to not see them as questions, but see them as a crucial element of the development and construction of a design. The brass utensil set IHADA he designed for FUTAGAMI has been a big seller since its launch. Before that, there had been few products in the market made of brass, because it's often considered risky to create objects made for daily use from this material. Without electroplating

or coating, the surface of brass will gradually change as time goes by. For the manufacturers, this means that they would have to deliver the product in uneven quality; for the customers, the product they've bought could change completely from what they purchased according to how they use it. It is a big problem to explain to customers these deviations in a product's quality. In fact, it can cause trouble in many aspects of production and sale, and so for a long time no one was interested in trying it. Knowing that FUTAGAMI is a company with an established history, which used to mainly produce objects for Buddhist temples, Oji thought, wouldn't it be charming if a daily commodity could be like something found in a buddhist temple? Changing with time means that it's unpredictable and unique; couldn't this be an interesting quality for utensils? Just like that, when seen from a different angle, a risky material has a new kind of appeal. Oji always tries to approach design with this attitude – design not to solve problems, but to fall in love with the problems that arise, and turn them into a different kind of asset.

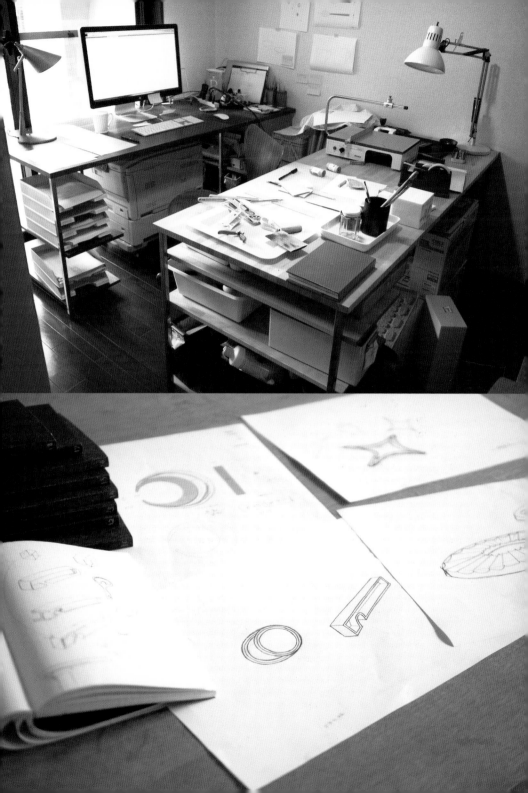

FUTAGAMI IHADA: butter knife, spice spoon, muddler / jam spoon.

JICON series porcelain tableware

KAKUDO series butter boxes

FUTAGAMI brass chopstick rests

KAMI series wooden plates

Artist

Nature is My Name

Jarek & Daria Berdak

Their love of nature, simple objects with souls, and woodcarving led to their handcrafted imperfect wares. Although a handcrafted piece might never be perfect, they pay close attention to details and work until they achieve the best results.

Jarek & Daria Berdak

Poland

Jarek and Daria Berdak are a couple working as a designer and a photographer in Warsaw, Poland. They established their customizable handmade wooden ware brand "I Love Nature" in 2010. Using materials like ash, oak and birch wood, their pieces are made with great care and their visible imperfections are a testimony of their handmade creations and highlight their uniqueness. www. ilovenature.pl

M orning in the deep mountain forests comes with the sounds of birds chirping and dogs barking, making the peaceful setting even more tranquil. This is the Berdak's workshop, in the mountains near Warsaw, the capital of Poland – a small cabin surrounded with fresh air, and filled with the couple's charm. It's a wooden house over 200 years old. Inside, there are all kinds of woodcarving tools with raw wood and utensils kept in a jumble inside and outside of the house. There is also disorder, with sawdust everywhere and dogs running from left to right. Without the need of an alarm or the sound of traffic, Jarek gets up early and writes down the ideas which come to him upon waking. That's how he starts his work every day.

Jarek's father, Jan Berdak, was a world-class artistic photographer and his mother was an actress in the theatre. Thus, Jarek grew up communing with art. As a child, he never could have foreseen that his life would have turned out like it has. When Jarek was a teenager, he attended private sculpting classes in which an old friend of his was an instructor, but even then he was deeply convinced that he would be a photographer just like his father. When he began his adult life he tried to follow in his father's footsteps and engaged in photography. After completing many culinary photo projects, he realized the passion was not there. Instead, he was in love with the cutting boards, utensils and tableware he shot. Jarek thought to himself, why not create the utensils himself? With this in mind, Jarek started working with wood and moved into the mountains. He found a house near the forest and built up his workshop, creating a handcrafted wooden tableware brand – I Love Nature.

"I Love Nature" as a concept is simple and clear, yet perfectly summarizes their creative goals. It was named after the Berdak couple's love of nature, their love of simple objects with souls, and their love of woodcarving. Jarek has handmade every piece in their collection throughout the production process. From choosing the wood to presenting the final result, he never puts his work into another's hands. He has a special approach to choosing wood and never goes to the mills or buys in bulk. Instead, he insists on sourcing raw material from nature for his sophisticated projects. Collecting wood from nature doesn't

mean harming the environment; one of Jarek's favorite hobbies is to take a walk around the forest and collect dead or discarded wood he comes across. Soiled logs from the stream, the wood from blown-down trees, old and demolished wooden houses, etc. are the perfect material for Jarek. Ash, walnut, maple and other hardwoods are Jarek's favorite raw materials. In addition to the reclaimed wood, Jarek also insists on using only old tools. He feels that new tools bought from stores have no soul. In his opinion, only by working with mature objects each with some history can he become a better man. The handcrafted ware created by Jarek are unique — each piece is the only one like it. Although a piece made by hand might never be perfect, Jarek is very meticulous in his work. He pays close attention to details and devotes a large amount of time to finishing every item. The detail work must be perfect, and he works only until he achieves outstanding results.

Most of Jarek's pieces are specifically designed for food, and when talking about his work or what they are intended for, Jarek always has much to share. The Berdak couple is obssessed with food in their daily life. Jarek says his entire existence revolves around food, meals, and planning for them. He likes spending the day waiting for the time when he can eat. Diversity and uniqueness in thinking up the daily menu is essential, and he enjoys experimenting with various cuisines. Because of this, the Berdak's home is full of culinary magazines and cookbooks.

The presentation of food with specific tableware is also a part of Jarek's work. Living in the mountains, he naturally takes care of the photography himself. Of course, it cannot be said that any wooden utensil will always be a perfect match for every kind of food; thus Jarek always imagines what a piece would look like paired with different kinds of food when he's creating a new piece. Working as a freelancer, he has always shared his life with his creative work. He would immediately be defensive if someone said to him that "Eating is just to appease hunger, why waste so much time on it?" Eating is an extraordinary pleasure for him. Tasting, finding new flavors and creating a meal are his favorite ways to spend his spare time. Food is a sensual and emotional experience, as well as a source of inspiration for Jarek.

Although Jarek loves to live in nature, he is far from a hermit isolated from the outside world. He lives with his wife, who shares the same beliefs regarding nature and food, and his dog, who always follows his master. He likes to share his work via the internet. In fact, when Jarek started creating wood utensils, his friends loved his work and shared it on social media, which got a great response in return and made Jarek decide to establish his own brand. After building up a website for "I love Nature," Jarek has received requests for custom-made tableware from around the world, which is exciting even if he feels somewhat conflicted. On the one hand, it gives him a feeling of satisfaction, as if a part of himself is travelling with the work around the world; on the other hand, requests for custom-made pieces can make him feel restrained, as he can be a very stubborn man when it comes to his creations. People often have private visions of what they want, and Jarek hates to compromise if his clients' opinions don't harmonize with his. "Be yourself, always, under any circumstances" is his motto. Thus he has to turn down orders every now and then. Jarek feels that maybe there are many people yearning for a life like his, but not everyone can coexist with nature like him. He is satisfied with his current living and working status, and doesn't want to change it in the future. He wishes to continue living his life in his own way, creating natural utensils for food with a natural attitude.

Artist

Embracing
the Simplicity of
Pottery

Li Le

The beauty of simple food wares lies in their natural lines and quietness. It is this natural simplicity that attracts people.

Li Le

China

Li Le, also known as Leziyan, is a designer and ceramist based in China. She graduated with a Master in Arts from Shanghai Theatre Academy. In 2010, she started to make ceramic ware, and established her studio "Jian Su Bao Pu". The series "Li" was exhibited at the Shanghai China International Arts Festivals in 2013 and 2014. weibo.com/imlile

Food is a paramount necessity for human beings and dining is an excellent occasion for people to get together, cementing the relationships between us. Beginning in ancient times, Chinese people have prepared their food according to the 24 solar terms every year. For any one of the 24 solar terms, people, especially the elders, would usually present specialty dishes served in particular tableware. These pieces might be simple or elaborate, but they've always been the supporting actors to food, which plays the leading role. The meal served in your average home might not be filling enough, but it's still something warm to share with family and friends. Li Le said she could still remember the warmth of the bowl of food her father saved for her in the cold winter when she was a child. This is what she could never forget – the warmth and flavors of home.

Li Le used to work as a graphic designer. Several years ago, she began to study pottery craft as a beginner, and eventually built up her own pottery workshop named "Jian Su Bao Pu" (meaning "Meet and Embrace the Simplicity") in Songjiang District, Shanghai. It was not easy to transition from being a professional in graphic design to a rookie in pottery who had to learn everything from the bottom up. At first, Li Le tried to align her ceramic products and the orientation of her branding with her conceptual perspective as a designer. But as she got to know more about pottery, the philosophy of her workshop started to change. She gradually gave up the commercial design perspective and started focusing on her own creative process. As time has passed, Li Le's workshop has also become a space for friends to gather.

For Li Le, the only standard of good tableware is "simple and natural." It is actually not that important whether or not the shape of a piece is innovative, if the decoration stands out, or it has multiple functions. In fact, there is no fixed standard to judge a certain piece, because different people appreciate different work in different moods or environments. Some people enjoy pragmatic pieces because they care more about their functions; some people enjoy work with an attractive appearance because they love the aesthetic. It's not necessary to set up a certain standard for that. The ceramic pieces Li Le loves are simple and natural, because pottery without much adornment has

A pottery bowl from the "Li" series

the power to become magically reassuring. As a pottery artist, Li Le always wishes to create something with the feeling of nature. That's what makes her work meaningful.

For Li Le, the most difficult part of pottery doesn't involve the techniques or skills, but accumulating experience with the kiln. Most of the time it wasn't the success in the kiln, but the failed experiences that improved her craft. Sometimes the aspects you can't control are the most difficult as well as the most interesting part of pottery creation.

In addition to creating and collecting ceramic ware, Li Le also loves to collect pieces made of different materials, such as glass, stone, iron, copper, and even leaves. She feels there are no limitations to the materials one can use for tableware. Even leaves, stone, bamboo, and the wood from the mountains and forests can brighten up our lives if we can feel them with our hearts. These vessels are the silent companions in our everyday lives.

Recently, Li Le has renovated an old house in Sanbao village in Jingdezhen and built up her second "Jian Su Bao Pu" workshop. Unlike the modern and always-busy Shanghai, the small and secluded village only attracts quiet potters concentrated on creating art. Every day, Li Le's work starts with checking the condition of the clay in production, moving some of it to staging areas in the sun and some back to the shade, fixing unsatisfactory pieces and glazing ones that are ready. After that, since Li Le still works as a creative director in graphic design, she spends some time dealing with the affairs of the design company. The rest of her time is mostly spent alone, thinking and studying. She usually begins working with clay or dealing with photography at dusk, when she finds herself to be most relaxed. Travelling back and forth between the two workshops in Shanghai and Jingdezhen is time-consuming and stressful, but Li Le is satisfied with her life. Just as the name of her workshops, "Jian Su Bao Pu," she is chasing her dream with an attitude of "taking things as they are." Staying in Jingdezhen on a regular basis has become a common occurance. Li Le says, "If you can learn from everything you experience, bit by bit, then everything can become an answer in your life." With this belief in mind, Li Le is on her way to pursuing her dreams.

"Jian Su Bao Pu" studio in Jingdezhen

A pottery bowl from the "Li" series

A tea bowl from the "Li" series

Bowls from the "Li" series

Artist

Memories in Blue

Michele Michael

The joy of working with clay is being able to experiment as she is making her ware. She enjoys making small batches of work and sending them out into the world when she feels they are ready.

Michele Michael

USA

Michele Michael is an independent ceramicist and founder of Elephant Ceramics Studio. She used to work as a stylist editor for an interior design magazine. In 2010 she started to work on handmade ceramics in her studio based in Maine. michelemichael.com

It is said that elephants have very good memories. Michele Michael's ceramic ware brand is named "Elephant Ceramics," and it's certainly memorable. The texture of Michele's work is created by a process involving pressing the clay with hand-woven linen; this, along with her distinctive color palette of varying shades of blue, green and white glaze, influenced by her surroundings in coastal Maine, lend a unique character to her work. Michele's style is somewhat rustic and imperfect in feel, and staying true to this "small-batch" mentality, she only makes one-of-a-kind pieces.

Earlier in life, Michele worked as a decorating editor for magazines and worked as a freelance prop stylist before opening a prop rental business in Manhattan. Her job throughout those roles was to seek out beautiful objects to tell a specific story. Immediately after graduating from college, Michele worked in a boutique in SOHO where one of her clients was a decorating editor at House & Garden magazine. This client hired Michele as her assistant, and knowing that Michele had studied fashion design in school, she told Michele that if

she was not interested in interior design and still wanted to pursue fashion design after a year, she would do her best to get Michele a staff position at Vogue magazine. To this day, Michele is not sure if that would have been possible, but it was an offer she couldn't refuse. Luckily for Michele, she discovered she loved the whole world of interior design. Starting a career in that kind of high-end, high-style environment influenced Michele's future choices and the kind of ceramics she creates today. Five years ago, she found a small local pottery studio in her neighborhood in Brooklyn, New York and started taking lessons. She fell in love with clay immediately. Two years ago, she decided to move to rural Maine and built a barn using timber from the local woods to serve as her studio. It's a traditional timber frame barn with a modern feel.

Living in rural Maine, Michele spends a great deal of time outdoors. She spends her time at the coast in the summertime, while in the winter, she loves to go for walks in the snowy woods. She finds inspiration in these sorts of activities in every season. A typical day for Michele is spent walking her three dogs

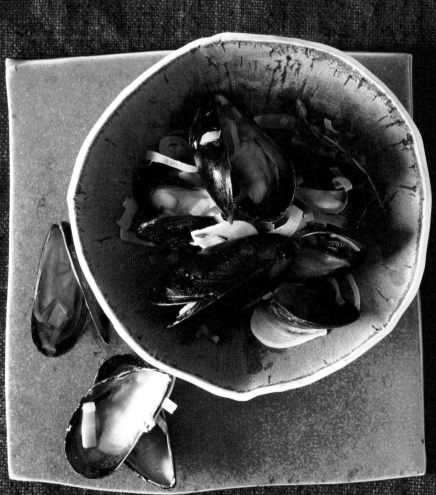

Pottery bowl and saucer in turquoise
Photography: Philip Ficks

Michele's work process
Photography: Stacey Cramp

along a country road, answering emails and correspondence, working in her studio for 4 to 5 hours, planning meals and events with friends, and cooking. Being a ceramicist, Michele prefers ceramics for her dishware, but she values glass for cold drinks and pottery for hot drinks, and she savors the feel of thinner, more delicate glass and pottery. Anything too heavy tends to distract from the enjoyment of eating and drinking. All in all, Michele likes simple, organic and handmade work where the food is not overwhelmed by the design of the piece. She strongly believes that tableware should enhance the food. She especially loves to use her friends' ceramics on her dining table with a mix of her own ceramics, along with vintage and new pieces she's collected. Michele doesn't care if the pieces match or not, as long as the color palette is similar. Daily meals provide a great source of inspiration for Michele's creative process.

The joy of working with clay for Michele is to be able to experiment as she is making her ware. The most interesting part of her work involves experimentation with glazing and creating new glazes, something Michele says she could never grow tired of. She feels she was never meant to be a production potter; she enjoys making small batches of work and sending them out into the world when she feels they are ready. Her work and her methods are a reflection of her motto and her attitude toward life: be happy in the moment.

Handmade shelves in Michele's studio

Photography: Stacey Cramp

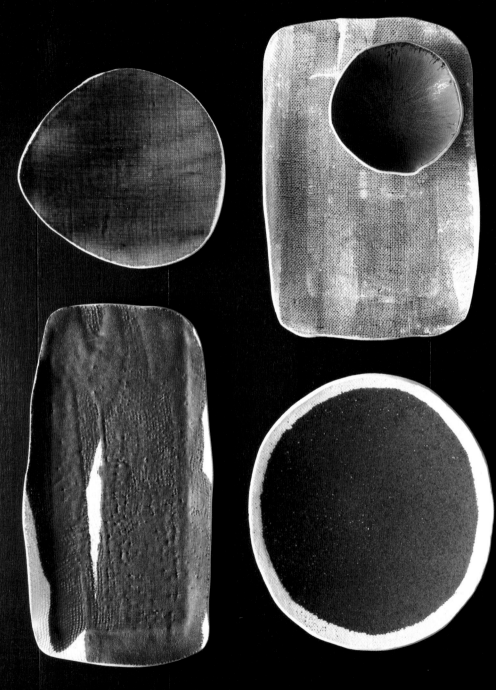

Bowls, platters and plates in shades of blue glaze

Brown Stoneware with an Ocean blue glaze
Photography: Philip Ficks

Stoneware platters and bowls in brown and white
Photography: Philip Ficks

The Soul of Tableware

Yumiko Iihoshi

The clean and glossy texture mimics the accuracy and consistency of volume production, while the exquisite shapes and cool colors unconsciously and quietly reveal the unique quality of handcrafting.

Yumiko Iihoshi

Japan

After graduating from Kyoto Saga University of Arts, with a major in porcelain, she started her own collection under the name "yumiko iihoshi porcelain". www.y-iihoshi-p.com

The first time you see Yumiko Iihoshi and her tableware pieces, words like quiet, comfortable, warm, and elegant come to mind. Even those who don't know much about art and design can tell that Yumiko's work feels "Japanese." Compared to Europe, America, and China, etc. where the emphasis is more on large scale commodities, the Japanese tend to emphasize small scale, precious items for daily use. As Japanese people tend to pay close attention to their food and health, they also express their particular aesthetics in the fine, smooth tableware they create. It's the power of silence.

Food is what keeps people alive, but mealtime traditions and culinary style are the elements that affect people's preferences. Your choices on the table speak right to your heart. As for Yumiko, food and tableware mean a tremendous amount in her daily life. If the tableware doesn't match the environment, you can't fully experience the beauty of the food, not to mention explore its place in your life.

Like many other ceramic artists, Yumiko started her career by building a kiln after graduating from the Ceramic Art department of Kyoto Saga University of Arts. When she first started her work, she found that many mass produced ceramic tableware pieces in the market were bright and easy to use, but most of them were filled with a coldness created by machines. You cannot feel their unique texture, which makes them uninteresting.

To create the most satisfying work, many artists focus on crafting their own pieces with a "unique trait," especially through working by hand. However, sometimes handcrafted pieces exist far removed from ordinary daily life because of the attitude that some people might have that it destroys art if they use them as normal everyday tableware. In this case, the wares are enshrined in a closet or on a shelf, which is inconsistent with the original purpose of creating useful things. Yumiko wants her work to be embraced by the general public, fit in naturally to any setting, and be welcome on every table. Only when used at the table does tableware fully reach the end of the process of creation. With the quality of high end mass production as well as their handcrafted texture, these pieces are meant to be both useful and beautiful, and that's what makes a good piece in Yumiko's mind. Isn't it a bold and innovative thought?
With this thought in mind, Yumiko pays close attention to not leave any handmade marks

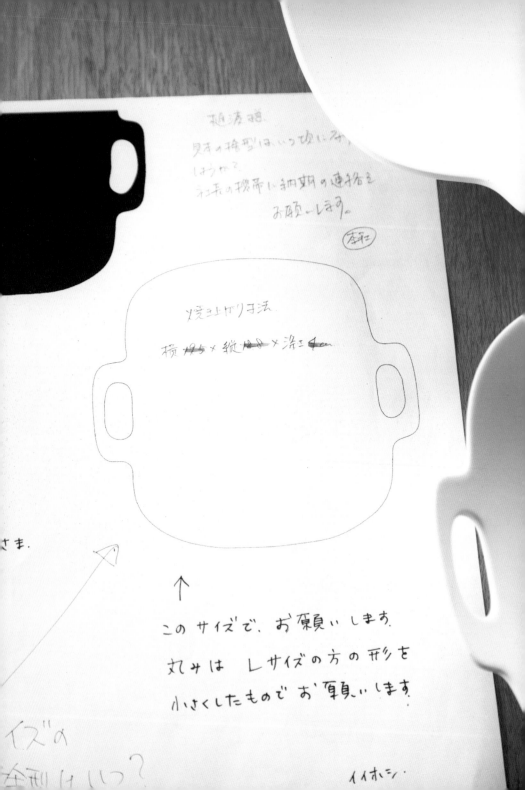

渡辺時
見本の挽型は、いつぱいにみ...
ほうか?
社長の携帯に納期の連絡を
お願いします。
（浅利）

メ完成上ガリ寸法.

横 ~~~ × 縦 ~~~ × 深工 ~~~.

さま.

↑

この サイズで、お願いします.

丸みは Lサイズ の方の 形を

小さくしたもので お願いします

イズの

型けいつ？

イイホシ.

during her creative process. After creating a piece she's satisfied with, she commissions local kilns in Japan for higher volume production. As for designing vessels for food, Yumiko usually avoids creating anything complicated or flaring. Instead, she always thinks about how to balance the color of the work with the color of the food which they would hold. Only pieces which are simple and concise, yet tender and elegant, can set off the natural beauty of food. Commissioning other people to produce one's creation is not an easy thing — Yumiko has to scrupulously communicate with the craftsmen about the design configurations, material proportions, color modulation, etc. before the actual production process begins.

Only after the procedure of molding, piece-making, and firing, does one find out if the production meets the expectations of the designer. The clean and glossy texture shows the accuracy and consistency of volume production, while the exquisite shapes and cool colors unconsciously and quietly reveal the unique quality of handcrafting. Able to flourish in different backgrounds or while serving different foods, the tableware meshes with a variety of styles; they are versatile enough to fit almost any environment and food, which is exactly the work Yumiko has always tried to create. The final pieces are representative of Yumiko's impressive spirit of persistently pursuing her ambition.

Many "new things" which have always been with us are in fact part of the "tradition" that people have always talked about. Ceramics is a traditional art with a profound history, but Yumiko is not bound by tradition or any other factors. Instead, she always finds inspiration from her own life and uses her own imagination for her creations.

Yumiko's studio is located in Tokyo, Japan; the space is not very large, but it's enough for a potter's wheel and kiln. Except for days when she's on business trips, Yumiko spends most of her time in the studio. She usually works alone, and when she's not working, her dog is her best companion. Yumiko intends to continue creating work the way she's always done, with each step followed by another step, and every move forward inspiring new goals and aspirations. Yumiko feels that although she is not a Christian, she has always lived her life with similar beliefs. She believes that the path is right in front of you, and you can only accomplish your own results when you ceaselessly walk along your own path. You can achieve anything if you really want it.

Artist

Totems:
Coffee, Tea and Soup

Luca Nichetto

Photography: Mjölk

Like exploring new foods, the process might be difficult,
especially when you encounter something that you don't like,
but it's always good to try.

Luca Nichetto

Italy

Luca Nichetto was born in 1976 in Venice. He earned his degree in industrial design at the Università
Iuav di Venezia. In 2006, he founded the multidisciplinary design studio Nichetto&Patners, and
works as an industrial designer and consultant. He has been awarded a number of international
prizes, such as EDIDA Designer of the Year award and the IF award. nichettostudio.com

F ood connects people. In any country, at any transitional point in its history, we can always learn more about it from its food than from other sources. The history, traditions, culture, and even the special character of each place can be traced through the food of local people: their flavors, ingredients, raw materials, popular dishes, etc. Italian designer Luca Nichetto loves to explore different cultures and traditions of other countries through his design. In 2014, he designed three collections of pottery ware: Sucabaruca, Aureola, and Cheburashka. Each series focuses on a different popular drink or food culture found around the world, namely, coffee, tea and soup.

Coffee is closely bound up with people's everyday life in Italy. In the morning, after meals, at work or in class, family and friends having gatherings – you can find Italians drinking coffee anytime, anywhere. There's an Italian saying: "una volta assaggiato il caffe italiano, non se ne vuole piu toccare nessun altro tipo." It means that once you've tasted Italian coffee, you'll never drink any other kind. Just like coffee in Western countries, tea tasting has a profound history in Asian countries. People say that Chinese tea has many similarities with Italian espresso; they both reflect the essence of the culture of their country through the traditions of raw material selection, processing, brewing, and sharing. Those who love coffee would probably be fascinated by the charm of tea. In modern times tea is not restricted to Asia, as people all over the world are soothed by and commonly drink the versatile beverage. Meanwhile, just like coffee and tea, soup is another international culinary culture that exists around the world. Although it takes many forms, soup is surely one of the most important dishes on people's dining tables.

As an Italian, Nichetto admires the traditional charm of the familiar drink of his country – that is to say, coffee. Nevertheless, Nichetto thinks that the methods of designing vessels for coffee, tea and soup are very similar due to their patterns of localization and globalization. For his series Sucabaruca, Aureola, and Cheburashka, he hid a secret surprise in every collection, in addition to the beautiful details and useful functions for serving coffee, tea and soup. When all the pieces of a collection are gathered together, they form a special

image which Nichetto calls a "totem" – a representative of culture. It might not be a message that everyone understands easily, but this almost sacred expression reveals Nichetto's love for these cultures.

Nichetto grew up in a small town on an island near Venice which is famous for its glass production. Ever since he was a kid, Nichetto had the chance to get in touch with glassmaking, and witnessed the production of many projects, from the early prototypes to actual products. Living in this environment filled with art and design, Nichetto naturally followed the path of an artistic life. Before college, Nichetto took a course in glasswork in an art academy. He saw how the students at that kind of school would usually prepare a portfolio with their paintings and visit the local factories one by one to promote their own designs, hoping that some of them would be appreciated by the buyers and put into production. Nichetto followed their example, promoting his work even until he was studying industrial design in college. He believes every attempted project beautiful; the process might be difficult, especially when you encounter something that you don't like, but it's always good to try. This works for exploring new food as well.

In regards to tableware design, Nichetto said he did not begin with any preference in materials. But as he implemented more projects from initial designs to the final product, he became fascinated with the excellent production techniques for pottery and ceramics. For his collection Aureola, Nichetto cooperated with a friend, pottery artist Lera Moiseeva, and commissioned Dymov Ceramic in Russia to produce the collection. Aureola was created with a traditional smoked kilning technique. After tempering on the potter's wheel and undergoing the desiccation procedure, the craftsmen would burnish the red clay by hand to remove the air pores. The finished pieces would then fired at 950 degrees centigrade in a custom-built sealed kiln, with wood shavings added for fuel. The decrease in atmospheric pressure enables a chemical reaction, which darkens the color of the clay. Last but not least, the pieces are polished with beeswax from local farms. Being produced with this kind of traditional technique, the vessels are full of Asian characteristics as well as sacred charm.

Cheburaska series tableware
Photography: Lera Moiseeva

Aureola tea set
Photography: Mjölk

Artist

Glass: A Journey
from Food to Tableware

Takeshi Tsujino

Any given piece might create a distinctively different atmosphere when it's moved to a new environment. It is very important for the artist to pay close attention to the relationship between space, the objects, and, naturally, people.

Takeshi Tsujino

Japan

Born in 1964, Takeshi Tsujino graduated from the Product Design Department of Osaka College of Design, and travelled and studied in the US thereafter. He returned to Japan and set up his own studio, Fresco. With more than 20 years of experience in hand blown glass, he is regarded as a master in this field. www.studio-fresco.com

The way Japanese people appreciate their meals is unique, as there is much emphasis on the freshness of the food. Back in the old days, the logistics of transporting anything were poor when compared to today. Therefore, freshness was a luxury for people. Creating a natural scene that would make people imagine the vegetables were just harvested, or foraged from a field and prepared a few minutes ago has always been seen as the height of hospitality and the proper way to treat a guest in Japanese culture. Takeshi Tsujino was interested in Japanese cuisine when he was young, and tried to become a chef, but the experience of being a cook made him realize that he was more interested in how the dishes were decorated than how to best flavor them, or serve a meal to diners. So he decided to turn his attention to creating three-dimensional works which would last longer than a lunch break. While Tsujino was on his quest to find a new direction, he ran into an exhibition that was showing contemporary glass art. The exhibition showcased glass pieces from all over the world, and they changed his idea of glass as a material.

Tsujino decided to devote himself to glass creation. After taking industrial design and glassmaking courses in Japan, he went to the US to continue his study of glass design. He spent a few years there and was baptized by the conceptual currents in the creative fields of the mid-80s. After graduating and coming back to Japan, he worked for a company that sold everyday items for several years, as handcrafted glass objects were rare in Japan in the early 90s, and he found he couldn't yet make a living out of handmade glass. Later, he was lucky enough to return to the glass business by working for an old company which produced colored glass canes for lamps. The company had a whole set of glass blowing equipment, but there was no one who knew how to blow glass in the company. Tsujino taught glass blowing classes, designed their production works, produced pieces, and worked on his private artwork. He worked for the company for 5 years until he could become independent and establish his glass studio, Fresco. He devoted two and a half years to building the living facilities, and six months to situating the workshop right next to the house. Now, Fresco has a 460-pound glass furnace, three work stations, some cold

Kasumi series plates

Spot series glasses

working equipment, and a gallery. There is also a small cafe next to the studio building where they can enjoy a cup of coffee at work.

Instead of referring to him as a designer, Tsujino prefers people call him an artist of glass. Fresco produces "craft products" which might be a little bit expensive for some people, thus the most difficult part of their work is to create the built in value. There are many galleries and stores that collect or sell their products. These places represent what Fresco really aims to achieve by creating the glassware, as production is not the ultimate goal of Fresco's mission. Tsujino would like to see ordinary people selecting their favorite handmade pieces and finding great enjoyment in them. So he tries to not just sell the objects, but to convey their vision of the world. Tsujino does not deal with galleries or stores which do not comprehend their mission. He says, "The most interesting part of being in this business is to see people who become more creative about using their products than they could ever imagine themselves being." The same piece might create a distinctively different atmosphere when it's moved to a new environment, which is very exciting for

Tsujino. It is very important for him to pay close attention to the relationship between space, the objects, and, naturally, people.

You must know the old in order to create the new. Tsujino is interested in things which have been on the market for a long time. "Long life design" is his aim when he tries to create something new. It might seem a little ironic for a glassmaker to say that, but Tsujino wants to produce things that will make people want to repair them if they are broken. There is a Japanese technique called "Kintsugi" which reconstructs broken ceramics or porcelains using Japanese lacquer and gold powder. When the broken utensils are repaired with this method, sometimes they become more beautiful than they used to be, and even more precious. The break reflects the attachment between the owner and the piece. Tsujino hasn't decided if he should produce "hard-to-break table wares," "repairable glassware," or not even think about the uncomfortable subject of broken glassware...

Outside of his craft, Tsujino enjoys surfing, motorcycle riding, hiking in the mountains, camping, and skiing, but he finds it difficult

to completely separate himself from work when he lives in the same building as his studio; his hobbies meld with his work in his constant search for the interesting things in everyday life, and musings about transforming experiences and items into glass. There is an old saying in Japan, "Bun Bu Ryo Do," meaning to pursue mastery in both martial arts and scholarship. Tsujino said he would like to follow this credo to grow as a glass blower continually and expand his skill in design. Running this unique business is difficult, and there is no one to go to for advice, but that's why it's worth the challenge.

Smaland series glassware

1.9m series small wine decanter

Pizca series glasses

Hibiki series plates

Artist

Timeless Tableware

Keiichi Tanaka

The passage of time can be remembered and expressed on clay vessels subtly. It is the charm of ceramics.

Keiichi Tanaka

Japan

Keiichi Tanaka is a ceramist born in Chiba, Japan in 1979. He graduated from the Department of Industrial, Interior and Craft of Musashino Art University. Now, he is an adjunct lecturer with the Faculty of Ceramic Design of Musashino Art University. keiichitanaka.com

The relation between food and eating utensils can be traced from ancient times. It's a custom unique to human beings when compared to animals; their development represents the development of food itself. In ancient times, food was only meant to alleviate people's hunger and they didn't bother with special tools to hold it. With the development of human civilization, food and utensils become necessary to each other. Those cooking began to make more beautiful and delicious food, and designers made more beautiful pieces to match different foods. Food and utensils have enriched people's lives and living environment.

Keiichi Tanaka's studio is located in his house, so he usually works at home. He likes cooking, not only because it is related to his creations, but also because he has recently become a father, and it's a wonderful way to spend quality time with his family. Tanaka's standard for choosing tableware is based on traditional Japanese culinary culture, such as using ceramics for daily use, but he prefers to use wooden dishes for soup, and glass tableware for cold foods. Besides this, he sometimes chooses irregular combinations according to the situation or dish. Sometimes he also chooses pieces with designs he himself would never make, because it's necessary in life to branch out to new experiences. One of Tanaka's standards in designing tableware is whether it would be useful or not; however, it is difficult to define what should be the standard for good use. He feels if a utensil inspires people to pick it up, then we can say it is a good one.

Tanaka has loved to create things since childhood, and it was no surprise that he decided to go to an art university. During college he was originally interested in interior, accessory and product design, and he wasn't interested in ceramics at all. But after he took a class about clay itself, in which he encountered Professor Makoto Komatsu (who later led him to his current career), he unexpectedly felt that this material suited him and decided to use it to express himself. Tanaka felt the infinite possibilities of ceramic design from Professor Makoto Komatsu's lectures, which expressed entirely different ideas than he had ever heard before. It led him to a new way of expressing himself through clay, one that reflects his deep love for cooking and eating.

Inspired by ironware and farm tools, Tanaka tried incorporating metal pieces into the clay of his works. Unexpectedly, the utensils produced in this method turned out to have a very unique kind of texture. Instead of reflecting the cold, hard sensations of metals, the clay mixed with metal revealed a nostalgic and warm atmosphere while retaining the softness and natural texture of pottery. The traditional craftsmanship of pottery production is beautiful and precious, undeniably vital to the art. However, sometimes it is necessary to weed out old traditions because craft should evolve from time to time alongside new trends. Tanaka feels that artists like himself who create new techniques should not forget that they exist on a base of tradition. He tries to pay tribute to the tradition of pottery production around the world with his creations. For example, in creating white glazed pieces, he was trying to reproduce the softness and smoothness of ancient painted pottery of the type which was widely circulated in Europe in the 15th and 16th centuries. When he created blue glazed work, he was trying to reproduce the typical blue glazing of the traditional pottery in ancient Egypt and Turkey. In addition, inspired by the environment and scenery of his hometown, Tanaka likes to create a certain kind of weathered and washed-out feeling in his work, as if it had existed for a very long time.

Tanaka's motto is "modesty." Utensils for food are one of the most ordinary tools in people's daily life. Based on the idea that they don't get to choose their users, rather people choose them, it is important for him to keep creating with modesty. Even though Tanaka is proud of his works, he doesn't think that he makes sublime works. He loves to see his creations being used by people every day, and become a part of their lives; that's the best part of his creation.

Artist

Playful Elegance

BCXSY

Cohen and Yamamoto like to maintain a constant flow of inspiration through their travel and collecting experiences. These are not necessarily design-related, but rather other activities which may inspire them – anything from nature to art, food, or meeting interesting people.

BCXSY

Netherlands

BCXSY is an Amsterdam-based interdisciplinary cooperative between designers Boaz Cohen (Israel, 1978) and Sayaka Yamamoto (Japan, 1984). BCXSY focuses on developing concept, identity, product, graphics, interior, and environmental projects. Offering a balanced combination of two unique talents, the studio delivers one distinct narrative that is characterized by an emphasis on personal experience, human interaction and emotional awareness. The artful intertwining of the specific or boutique with the universal and commercial is the hallmark of the BCXSY design experience. www.bcxsy.com

The most attractive aspect of handblown glass is the delicate balance between perfect and imperfect. This balance reflects the characteristics of glass, as well as the level of the artist's skill. Glass pieces may seem identical at first glance, but if you look more carefully you will find subtle differences in their shapes, colors, and sizes, etc. Every piece is unique. Likewise, the charm of ceramics lies in the natural beauty of the material, as well as the potter's technique and attention to detail. All of these aspects create infinite possibilities in the art of handcrafting. Pursuing both aesthetic value and functionality, the glass and ceramic ware created by Dutch and Japanese duo BCXSY is fresh, elegant, and playful.

BCXSY is short for Boaz Cohen X Sayaka Yamamoto. The couple's design work is famous for its maverick playfulness. Function over form has always been one of the most influential beliefs in modern design, whether in architecture, graphic design or handicrafts. Yet against the background of modern society, with its increasingly abundant material commodities, pure functionality can no longer satisfy the ever-changing needs of constant consumption. BCXSY's design is rich in form

and color, as well as sense of humor, which always attracts people's attention. Cohen and Yamamoto say they don't make a concerted effort to define their style, but rather try to concentrate on further development, following their instincts and personal preferences.

Cohen and Yamamoto like to maintain a constant flow of inspiration through their travel and collecting experiences. These are not necessarily design-related, but rather other activities which may inspire them – anything from nature to art, food, or meeting interesting people. This is part of the process of turning imagined work into a tangible product – experiencing that which is genuine, such as scenery, artwork, interesting people and all of the various kinds of food that one would encounter during a trip. Food is one of the greatest pleasures in life for these two – they both love cooking and exploring new flavors, ingredients, etc. They also feel that food is one of the most exciting ways to learn about a new culture or environment while traveling.

In Between is a collection of glassware designed by BCXSY and produced by glass studio Fresco. The cups, bowls, saucers and more were

Origin part IV: Foster ceramic pieces

presented in 6 gradients, from transparent to entirely white, all of which were produced with handblown glass. In order to realize this kind of gradient, craftsmen added different quantities of white pigment during the production of every piece, instead of adopting the common abrasive blasting technique. The pottery series Foster was created in collaboration with the young craftsmen of Ibuki Studio of Takumi Juku in Kyoto, Japan.

When creating pieces for food, Cohen and Yamamoto usually prefer working with natural materials. They think that there's good reason for using materials such as glass or ceramics for the creation of tableware that will be in contact with food. There are many factors to consider when thinking of the eating experience and further use – not only the visual aspects, but also durability, hygiene, etc. Materials such as glass or ceramics are therefore quite ideal: aside from being tough and easy to clean, they also offer endless possibilities when it comes to form and application.

Cohen and Yamamoto's creations have never deviated from their personal style. They tend to choose rather simple tableware and avoid very specific pieces in their own life, such as pieces specially designed for one type of dish. Since they also care about the presentation of food, they see food and creativity as strongly connected. This means that a plain piece of tableware should serve as a canvas for the meal, rather than having too much of a direct influence on the experience. Food is the main attraction.

In Between series — gradation
Photography: Kiyotoshi Takashima

Stories of the Craft

Time precipitates life. When we talk
about design, we're also talking about the inherent
meaning in a piece of work.
When you find an artistic discipline that you
would like to succeed in and dedicate yourself to,
design becomes a lifestyle and habit, imperceptibly
changing the connotations of your work. And
as for our designers, what have they dedicated
themselves to? Join us in exploring their
stories about their craft.

Beauty from the Earth

Kirstie van Noort

She has developed her own system to test all of the colors "purely" or "mixed" — with each other in different proportions, just like color modulation in painting. She changes the proportions for different results and never tires of it.

Kirstie van Noort

Netherlands

Dutch ceramist Kirstie van Noort was born in 1986. During her education in the Design Academy Eindhoven, she was studied under the famous ceramist Frans Ottink. In 2011, she graduated and set up her studio, focusing on communicating a certain process or the story behind a material. kirstievannoort.nl

Littlejohn's Clay Pit in St Austell, UK
Photography: Xandra van der Eijk

The clay for porcelain production comes from the earth and eventually settles in our daily lives. There are many beautiful ceramic pieces on the market, painstakingly decorated by designers. The glaze covers the original colors and textures of the clay, which makes diverse palettes and patterns possible. While many artists try to cover the original colors of the clay, Dutch designer Kirstie van Noort is obsessed with exploring them. She strives to make the original colors of the earth the final colors of the pieces she designs.

Kirstie took her first ceramic class from Dutch ceramist Frans Ottink while attending university in 2008; this is where she learned how to work with color and porcelain. She was fascinated by the raw material of porcelain – it is very light, almost white in color, and one can make almost any color with it. At the time, Kirstie was convinced that she would become a designer focused on creating gorgeous and exquisite porcelain pieces. But a trip she took before graduation entirely changed her career path. For her graduation project in 2010, Kirstie was free to choose

Hendra Pit in St Austell, UK

any topic. She decided to go to Cornwall, UK, home to many clay pits, to see and learn everything about the production process of porcelain. She learned that if you want to create 1 kilo of perfect white clay, you have to produce 6 kilos of waste. This waste is not reused in production; if lucky, it might be used for fixing roads or building houses. But most of the time it would simply be discarded randomly around the pits or factories. On the same trip, Kirstie saw colors of earth that she had never seen before. She decided to experiment with the waste leftover from

the production process, and began to collect different samples from different pits and factories. Traveling through Cornwall, Kirstie saw all types of mines, such as copper and tin. Next to these mines there were also large fields of "colored earth." She took 150 kilos of material back home, and there the research started.

For the project Ceramic Paint Collection Cornwall, Kirstie travelled to Cornwall twice and collected material from waste fields, then mixed the materials once she arrived back

Ceramic samples collected

at her atelier. Kirstie has developed her own system for doing this. First, she tests all of the colors "purely," without mixing them with any others. After that, she chooses colors to mix with each other in different proportions, just like color modulation in painting. It may sound easy, but the procedure requires a great deal of patience and a large amount of time, along with a professional knowledge of clay. The experiments and records of "mixing" constitute Kirstie's color palette. These records reveal the steps that Kirstie took to create a certain color – from dark to light, or the other way around.

Along with her research, Kirstie also creates pieces with the materials she collects. Unlike the usual tablewear made of white clay and glazed with industrial paints, Kirstie's work is filled with unique, natural colors from the earth. The colors of her pieces have become a characteristic of her work. As an artist, Kirstie finds the most interesting part of her work to be the research itself rather than developing more product lines, because it enables her to work with a material in a way that people don't recognize or expect. For example, her 6:1 project is about how to use the waste from the porcelain industry to create a new bowl or cup.

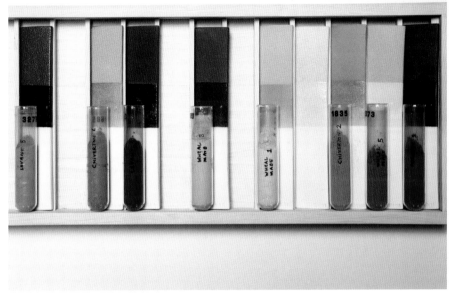

Color chart with different colors

When she discovered during her research that it was possible, she wanted to experiment more and more. Currently, Kirstie is busy with four different projects, and she recently travelled back to Cornwall to collect more unique materials. She says that if she discovers 50 new places, 50 new colors will follow. Her goal is to test every color that she encounters, and to eventually create a new book and a collection.

Un-kilning color chart sample

Utensils created with the wasted material from the 6:1 Project

Story

The Romance of Life

Lilah Horwitz

To believe in possibilities and imagination, and following your heart. The most beautiful work in the world is generally attributed to the simplest of ideas.

Lilah Horwitz

USA

Lilah Horwitz is a fashion designer, craftsman, and ceramist. She graduated from Parsons School of Design and works across Milwaukee, New York and West Virginia. She enjoys a self-described slow nomad life with her partner Nick Olson, who is a photographer, designing unique handmade clothing and selling it online. www.lilahhorwitz.com

Lilah and Nick's glass cabin
Photography: Jordan Long, Matt Glass

Before noticing Lilah Horwitz's tableware creations, we were fascinated by her dream-like glass cabin, which she built together with her husband, Nick. They built the cabin on a whim. On one of Lilah and Nick's first dates, Nick took Lilah to his family's land in West Virginia. They were sitting up on the hill where the house is now, watching the sunset, and joking about how wild it would be to build a house made up of only windows. Six months later, they packed up their belongings, moved down to West Virginia, and built that house. It was hard, crazy, and completely liberating.

Lilah says that it's a beautiful feeling to know that you built the roof over your head. The home is furnished with a mix of vintage furniture they had collected over the years and furniture they built with their own hands. They often use the porch as their dining table and set it with the ceramics and wooden bowls they have made. They keep a small garden in West Virginia, and both find it immensely fulfilling to eat food they have grown, from the plates they have made, on a table that they've built. Their life in West Virginia has always been an adventure. It's a beautiful place to go when they need time to dream and be close to

Lilah and Nick
Photography: Naomi Huober

the land. Lilah's favorite thing to do there is watch the lunar cycle, full moon to full moon. That is the true way to measure a month.

Lilah grew up beside her mother in the garden and her father in his woodshop. Her family's food came from their own backyard, and the house was an eclectic mix of found objects and beautiful things created by her father. She has always been surrounded by an incredible amount of creativity; one of her earliest memories is of finger painting the kitchen floor with her mother. From an early age, she was taught that one could produce anything for themselves, whether a table to eat on or the meals to eat on it. Food means relationships to Lilah: It's the relationships with farmers, vendors, friends, family, people's hands and the earth. Food is a center point for community and culture, a delicious moment in everyday life. For Lilah, setting the dining table is like a performance. There are many characters that contribute to a meal. Aesthetics can be equally as important as taste. Small beauties can be found in the daily task of eating, and sometimes Lilah's breakfast table becomes a great work of art.

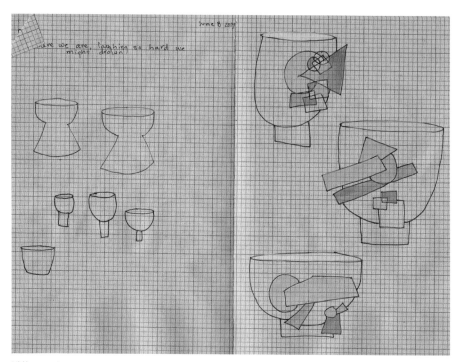

Lilah's manuscripts

Lilah went to Parsons School of Design, where she studied fashion design and sustainable design in the Integrated Design Program. Her practice began to take on more conceptual ideas in addition to form and function. After working solely with textiles for four years, Lilah ventured back into the ceramics studio and began creating objects with a more conscious design in mind. This was a return to the craft for her, as Lilah began working with clay when she was 8 years old. She had a wonderful mentor, a passionate and talented woman who took Lilah under her wing and cultivated in her a love of working with her hands. Lilah began creating tableware at a young age, but at that time she was more passionate about throwing the pots on the wheel than with the final result.

Lilah's process is very fluid and hands-on. There is often a loose sketch or drawing, then a form evolves from the clay, sometimes evoking the drawing, sometimes not. Lilah appreciates both primitive and modern styles in ceramics. She often finds that she borrows design practices from many cultures, sometimes seeking inspiration in ancient earthenware, other times in the lines of Brancusi's sculpture.

Lilah makes pieces that are pleasant to the eye, yet still challenging to the viewer. She hopes to encourage people to think of everyday objects as both functional and as works of art.

Lilah's studio practice focuses on ceramics and textiles, while Nick concentrates on woodworking and tintype photography. There is great crossover between their work when they collaborate, and the result is always exciting; for instance, she has collaborated with Nick on ceramic vessels that are rounded at the base and have corresponding wooden shapes in which they are designed to fit perfectly.

Lilah works mostly in high fire stoneware, and she thinks a lot about the materiality of wood and clay – both natural materials from very different sources, yet which relate to each other so nicely both in the studio and in nature.

Aside from their work together and artistic creation, Lilah and Nick are very romantic in life. Once, when Lilah was in New York City, Nick mailed her a box filled with beautiful bird nests. He had been clearing trees in the woods in Wisconsin during the winter; and found several abandoned bird nests and knew they would be a perfect gift for Lilah. Ever

Handmade spoons
Photography: Naomi Huober

since Lilah and Nick met and started working as a pair, their studio has moved with them as they travel. Sometimes it is in their home, sometimes in a shared studio, sometimes on the dashboard of their truck! One of their shared hobbies is what they call a "paper walk," where they walk a certain distance and collect all the pieces of paper they find on the street along the way. It's graphically very interesting to see the paper trail of a neighborhood.

Lilah often dreams up a design and has to force herself to slow down in order to execute it. She gets incredibly excited every time she sees her ideas realized in clay! Working on many pieces at once helps her feel as though she's always making progress. Her belief is that on many occasions, the most beautiful creations in this world come from the simplest acts of the heart. If love is at the core of your work, you can do no wrong. Lilah believes that we must make the world we want to live in. And that is exactly what she intends to do!

Handmade wares
Photography: Naomi Huober

Lilah's ceramic wares and Nick's wooden wares together with Brian Carpenter's artwork on an old coffee table

Photography: Nick Olson

Handmade vases

Photography: Nick Olson

Story

A Spoon a Day

Stian Korntved Ruud

He experiments like a scientist with the quantitative and variable properties to exhaust all the possibilities, draw a conclusion, and find the best solution.

Stian Korntved Ruud

Norway

Norwegian designer Stian Korntved Ruud was born in 1989. Through his innate fascination with how products are made and put together, Stain has always experimented with, modified, repaired and destroyed the objects around him. His works have been widely awarded and exhibited in Norway, France, America, the UK, Italy, Germany, Sweden and more. www.stiankorntvedruud.com

Stain picking suitable material from the forests near his studio

In Norway, wood is considered a reliable, profound, integrated, and warm material, which makes it one of the most frequently-used raw materials. Norwegian designer Stian Korntved Ruud loves working with wood. Like most Norwegian designers one might imagine, Stian is natural, modest, amiable, consistent, and creative. With the pure goal of improving his wood carving skills, Stian started his "Daily Spoon" project with the intention of continuing it for an entire year. His aim was to challenge and explore a spoon's aesthetic and functional qualities. Beginning with his first spoon, completed on March 26th, 2014, Stian solidified his determination to make a new spoon every day for the following 365 days. Stian accomplished his "Daily Spoon" project in March 2015 with every spoon completed. Each spoon he created for the project took a different size and shape, and displayed different functions and characteristics. Nevertheless, all of the spoons remained essentially the same despite apparent differences. Stian's work embodies his unconstrained imagination, which serves to widen people's horizons and perceptions of what tableware can be.

How long is a year? 12 months, 52 weeks,

365 days. To think of a feasible design project and implement it every single day is not a simple thing. Stian said, "It's easy to come up with lots of ideas, but to filter out the good ones and realize them physically are the most difficult parts of the task." Making a small item like a spoon looks simple, but from the modeling, design and raw material selection, to the carving process, none of it is easy; not to mention that he had to finish every piece within one day, without any repetition, in 365 days. The "Daily Spoon" project was not only a challenge for Stian, but also an experiment; different kinds of wood and different shapes could be turned into infinite possibilities. Trying to break through the restrictions and sticking to the fundamentals in innovation are one type of experimentation, like equations, ratios, and variables in science. In attempting to convert his ideas into as many variations as possible, Stian found the best solutions through this process. He made all the spoons in a traditional way with only hand tools, which was the constant variable in his "experiment," along with the material; Stian likes working with wood, and he often went to the forest to pick the wood that he liked most for each project.

The more pragmatic and simple an item is, the less it changes with the passage of time. It might not become a classic, but it has the potential to be inherited through generations and possibly last forever. Spoons – pure, simple and useful – have existed since ancient times, and people have used them for over 7000 years. This simple utensil has witnessed the history of human beings from the age of barbarism to civilization. The spoon has a pure, simple function, but it remains closely related to the general public, which is one of the reasons Stian chose it as the form for his experiment. After finishing a spoon every day,

Stian would take a photo of the new piece and then put it in a box with the others, waiting for the last spoon to be carved. He has no specific production plans for his spoons; in fact, he is not a designer who specializes in utensil design, he does not even focus on wood in his usual work. Nevertheless, the "Daily Spoon" project has inspired him to develop his other design skills in ways he could never have predicted.

Story

Delicious Tableware

mischer'traxler

Their unconventional wares designed with fruits and vegetables delight everyone. Balancing good design with whimsy to bring a smile to our faces.

mischer'traxler

Austria

Katharina Mischer (1982) and Thomas Traxler (1981) formed mischer'traxler studio. Based in Vienna they develop and design objects, furniture, processes, installations and more, thereby focusing on experiments and conceptual thinking within a given context. www.mischertraxler.com

When we look at the bowls created by mischer'traxler, it's just like looking at food itself. Some people say, simplicity is the key to beauty; the best utensil is one which people can easily tell its function at a glance. Some say they should quietly set off the beauty of food, otherwise it would be like a presumptuous guest usurping the host's role. In fact, everyone has his or her own preference in choosing their daily ware. When mischer'traxler's typical pieces lay quietly on the dining table, their colorful and interesting appearances brighten the whole room, easing the tension of busy urban life, and

helping to bring back a state of innocence.

Founded by Katharina Mischer and Thomas Traxler, mischer'traxler has always been a studio that experiments with interesting projects. Katharina and Thomas say they like to express the beauty of daily life in their works through a figurative approach. They're obsessed with experimental, conceptual, and analytical design projects. Their starting point was to make "fruit-bowls" out of real fruit and leftovers, but all of the material tests failed or didn't satisfy them. They were starting to become frustrated when

they looked at a bowl of fruit and realized that the shape between the fruit and the bowl itself was creating a negative imprint, which could in turn function like a bowl and reveal the details of the fruit. After multiple material tests, they finally found a way to produce a small number of pieces. After two years of work they were able to put the bowls into higher-volume production. It's incredibly satisfying for them to see their experimental project become a durable, dishwasher-safe, and so to say, "real" product available for the general public.

This series of vessels with the shapes of fruits and vegetables is called "Reversed Volumes." The prototype was produced using real fruits and vegetables. By pouring the molding material for pottery production between the bottom bowl and the real fruit or vegetable, a preliminary article could be taken out after the pouring material hardened. The coloring procedure is one of the key points in production. The custom-made argil powder perfectly reproduces the appearance of the fruits and vegetables like realistic paintings. Together with the "duplicated" shapes, all the

Color tests for reversed volumes

details of the healthy and delicious fruits and vegetables come to life.

Katharina and Thomas said that retaining the exact shape of the piece from modeling through firing was the most difficult process to realize.

Dishes are the complements to food. For Katharina and Thomas, tradition is something very valuable and also very regional and specific – so they try to treat it with sensitivity. Traditions should be cherished and the knowledge of how to do things should not be lost. At the same time, in order to keep tradition alive, it is necessary to adapt some of them to fit it into the 21st century – otherwise they would get lost. Some can be combined with modern technology, contemporary themes or with new views on social issues or telling the story of their creation. By now, mischer'traxler has realized over 10 kinds of fruit and vegetable pieces, including apple, lemon, orange, cherimoya, pimento, eggplant, pak choi, muskmelon, broccoli, and cabbage, etc. These bowls vividly duplicate the original appearance of the food, filling the quiet dining table with renewed energy, revealing a special beauty different from traditional ceramics.

Modeling of cauliflower

All ten bowls

(Left) Cherimoya | (Right) Cabbage

Postscript

Good food and lovely tableware go hand-in-hand, much like the subjects of art and literature. I studied art for many years, and I myself have designed some tableware for food and tea-tasting. Every time I see beautiful utensils, I can't help but appreciate and, ultimately, collect them. Although I'm often busy with my work and don't have much time to take care of my collection, my wife, who loves tea-tasting, and my mother, who loves cooking, always make good use of the beautiful pieces. They express their philosophy of life through small daily details, which inspires me while making me feel a little bit guilty for not doing so myself.

One of my warmest memories is of a sweet holiday with my family in early spring. The weather was chilly, but we were sitting in the living room, watching TV, drinking cups of fresh, warm tea, chatting with each other, while my mother prepared lunch for us. When lunch was ready we all gathered around the table, savoring the simple but delicious home cooking. I've always been busy with my work since I hold several posts simultaneously; I'm lucky I have my family, in which everyone lives their life to the fullest. What more could a man ask for? I guess this was the original inspiration for making a book about food, tableware, and life.

Over the past year and a half, our team has interviewed over a dozen designers and creators who love food and tableware, many from different countries, working in different mediums. We're very grateful for all of the designers who have participated in this book; without their support, we wouldn't have been able to share so many wonderful stories. Many of the anecdotes and projects in this book have never appeared in print before. During my communications with designers, many times I simply listened to their stories. In most cases I found myself sharing their feelings. It was like talking to someone you've just met, but quickly feeling like you've known them for a long time. When talking about "a favorite piece of work," the answers of many of the designers were not a classic work of some design master or some luxury piece that one would be too nervous to use, but a simple and common utensil in their daily life. For example, Takeshi Tsujino's favorite piece is a mug on his workbench which he uses every day; Yumiko Iihoshi's favorite piece is the large bowl that she's used for many years, unwilling to get a new one; Keiichi Tanaka's favorite is the series of French dishes which he unexpectedly came across during a trip to France. The destiny of a piece of tableware is ultimately decided by the people who use it. Talking with these designers, who love utensils and love life, always filled me with positive energy.

For the past ten years, we have been publishing books with a global view, exploring and excavating the macroscopic meaning of concept and design. With the development of the Internet as a sharing platform, information is now expanding at an unexpected rate; however, or maybe because of this, more and more people are starting to pay attention to the common beauty of daily life. In preparing for this new book, we were warmly supported by many excellent designers as well as young editors and book designers and their teams, which we're incredibly thankful for. We are also very grateful to many other people whose names do not appear in the credits, but who made specific contributions and provided support. Due to the limited space available, some interviewed designers' works and stories were not able to be featured, for which we are truly sorry. We will continue digging deep into the field of lifestyle design aesthetics, and hopefully our readers will continue to enjoy our publications.

Wang Shaoqiang
Chief Editor